S0-BAQ-254

Over a Cup of Coffee

Some thoughts

Some ideas

Some reflections

Some questions

Some love

Some lessons

A sum

Of experiences

An effort

To inspire

Contemplation

Acknowledgments

The idea of this book was conceived at Toastmasters, an international organization that helps develop communication and leadership skills, as I started giving speeches. I have enjoyed many interesting conversations over the years and it felt right to start noting the concepts to encourage contemplation. This book is my first attempt at writing. It is a collection of ideas and reflections on life, presented in an informal, friendly, light manner, like friends talking over a cup of coffee.

I am deeply grateful to my family who have inspired and encouraged my intellectual curiosity; my daughter Ashna who teaches me something new every day, my husband Pranav who has so lovingly and patiently lived the journey; deepest thanks and gratitude to my brother Dr. Anurag (Anubhai) Gumashta who has been the harbinger for this creation; my parents Dr. Gita and Dr. Prafullakumar Gumashta who have inculcated ideas for contemplation and shared spiritual journey; my parents-in-law Raksha and Dr. Bhupen Trivedi for their continued love and support, my sis-in-law and friend Ranak & Vibhor Chhabra who have shared my fears and successes.

I am especially thankful to all my loved friends and colleagues for sharing their experiences which have inspired a topic.

I am grateful to my editor Karen from Create Space.

Finally, I would like to thank my God Krushna. With deep humility I present this in His feet.

*This book is dedicated to my brother Dr. Anurag, my husband
Pranav and my God Krushna*

Contents

1. The Concept of Distance

Ever since my childhood, I have been overly attached to my family and my country, India. I never wanted to leave India. Like most of us, I wanted to stay in my "comfort zone" around my family, thinking that someday I would be able to be there for them.

However, time proved that I am indeed not "here" but "there," and yet *I am there* for them. Knowing me too well, my brother started this conversation with me—over a cup of coffee.

Distances exist more in the psyche than in the physical world. You can feel close—and be close—to someone even if you are miles apart, and you can live next door to someone and yet be distant. Proximity may help in staying connected, but it does not guarantee closeness.

Geographical distances should not matter in relationships. It does take effort to stay in touch with friends who live far away; after all, you won't typically bump into each other in parties or at the mall. Then, when you are living apart, whether it's twenty miles or twenty thousand miles, geographical distances will be just relative to time—so instead of driving twenty miles, you may take an eighteen-hour flight to meet them.

But…is it really so? Is it really so with everybody? Doesn't it happen that one fine day you realize you are not a part of their daily lives but just a part of major events? That said, do you really want to be—and is it really necessary to be—a part of their daily lives? To know what happened in the office, whether they got stuck in traffic or held up due to the weather?

I think if we actually want to be in touch with others, the current means of communication available—social media, Internet, and phones—make it very easy. Sometimes, distances can even help with getting close. My parents have commented that my relationship with them has improved because of the distance; before, we used to just take each other for granted.

There is no doubt that physical distances exist; it's how we use the distance to build closeness that counts.

Don't
Build distances
Build bridges
Of love
Of forgiveness
Of trust
Of being there

Let
Physical distances
Not be
Distances
Of the heart

2. The Circle of Friends

In continuation of the previous discussion, this is a conversation I had with Daddu (my father-in-law), a very well-read, intelligent, and inspiring person.

Each of us has various concentric circles with our close ones, with "you" at the core. The innermost circle is that of your family—it is usually the closest one (though not necessarily). With this circle, you are involved in the day-to-day or week-to-week affairs. I call my innermost circle my "legal advisors," consisting of me, my husband, one friend, one of my parents, one of my siblings, and God; and each one of us has a vote. So, when I am facing a confusing issue, my legal advisors help me find a resolution. Sometimes they end up confusing me even more...and when that happens, my vote (and God's) wins out.

Even professionally, it is a good idea to have a "trust group," consisting of one friend who supports us no matter what, one person who can give us honest feedback, one person who opposes our views and one mentor who can guide us on how we should express ourselves, give words to our wisdom. When we run our ideas past the trust group, we will get a taste of how they will be received.

As we move farther out from the core, in concentric circles of relationships our involvement in the daily lives and heart-to-heart secrets becomes fewer and fewer. Friends—or, sometimes, even perfect strangers—can skip these concentric circles and come nearer to the core. When this happens, it may give us either joy or sorrow—especially if we are not ready to accept the changes.

As my father used to remind us, "You don't choose your family, but you can always choose your friends."

Scriptures in India and many other religious texts say, in some shape or form, that you should love everybody and feel a oneness with all. They say we should see God in all things, as everybody is a part of God. Does that mean that for such saints there are no concentric circles? Does that mean that they live the concept of "I am God" or "I am"? Or, as I am God and everything is created by God and everything dwells in God, does that mean "I am it"?

I haven't reached that state, though I am sure that then all concentric circles would merge into one dot—you or God.

A drop
A circle
Existence

A drop
Another drop
Travel
Growth

A circle
And a circle
Encircling
Peace

A point
A circle
A drop
In the ocean
Immortality

3: The Power of Choice

I really like the words "choice" and "free will." There is choice and then there is destiny. Choice is so inherent to the concept, or rather the power/feeling, of freedom in mankind.

Memories of the past
Facts of the present
Apprehensions of the future
And me
Wondering
Wandering

Options and choices
Choices and consequences
Consequences and the course of life
And me
Wondering
Wandering

Yes, everything is a choice, and choices do have consequences. Consequences are also a gift package, and you have to accept the whole deal! I find it amusing how we like to complain about some aspect of the consequences of our choices—like if we choose to live in a lovely, vibrant city like Chicago, we have to accept its harsh winters. Complaining about the consequence doesn't help, does it?

I have always believed this: if you make a decision, don't change it and don't regret it. To stand by a decision helps you become firm and courageous. I dislike the idea of being on the fence, being wishy-washy about things. I like making choices; and I have, over time, developed the courage to accept the consequences of those choices.

And then

Within my chosen environment and consequent circumstances
I stand perplexed
I had chosen this—hadn't I?

My choice has become my bondage
And they tell me to compromise
Compromise freedom for security
Compromise adventure for money
Compromise the jest of living for the fear of failure
Compromise the power to choose and instead become choiceless

I have another choice today…

4: The Alive Dead

A quote from my brother Dr. Anurag, "I enjoy the company of dead authors better than the people who are alive and yet dead." To further quote his poem:

Dying—gradually, futilely
Time has added the years
To the sum total of a broken scarecrow

Dishonored promises
Despised life
Chronic suffering

A withered bud
Unaware of the poisoned soil
Wonders
Where has the capacity to blossom disappeared?

I have a colleague at work and all I hear him do is complain—complain about the company, the work, his boss, his commute, the weather, TV soap operas...just about everything. As I think of him and the time he spends complaining, I am reminded of the "alive dead." Indeed, at such times, dead authors would be much better company!

We have all seen the living dead. As I took a minute to look around, I thought, *How many people show joy on their faces? Isn't being alive today a good thing? Aren't you happy just to be given an additional day?* Indeed, where has our capacity to blossom gone? Why have we all become, in some way, the "alive dead"?

I promise to be "alive" in the true sense—to live life to its fullest, to stop brooding over the past or worrying about the future and instead living the present moment.

Today is new
And so is this moment
And just as new is our endeavor
To live life
Agile and joyous
Awake and conscious
Let's rise to a new morning

5: Why *Not* Me?

The credit of this thought goes to my office friend, Joy. Joy had been diagnosed with breast cancer and had undergone the whole ordeal of chemotherapy and radiation. She is only thirty-eight. Just last quarter she had a relapse. It was hard the first time, and I think it is harder the second time. I wonder if knowing the pain you may have to go through makes it easier or tougher. Or maybe it just depends on your state of mind at that point in time.

In any case, we all in such circumstances tend to think, "Why me—why am I to suffer like this?" However, Joy thinks, "Why not me—why am I so special as to not get this? Am I the best person in the world? Would I rather any child have this? No, never! Would I rather trade this with a granny who is already suffering from a plethora of other problems? No, that wouldn't be fair. Then, why not me?"

I think that God likes to test his strong children, knowing fully well that they will clear his test. I remember a historical incident that has always amazed me. It is from the Hindu religious text *Shrimad Bhagwat*, where Kunti, the mother of the Pandavas who was also related to Lord Krushna, is blessed with the opportunity to ask for a boon. She requests God to give her suffering because during sorrowful times she always remembers God, and He has always protected her and her family. She feels his presence.

So, why not me? And why not you?

Why me?
Or
Why not me?

I have sinned
I have lied
I have hurt
Why not me?

Let it be
I can survive
I will live
Let it be me

6. I, Me, Myself Time

I had this discussion with multiple people, including my sis-in-law (who also has a PhD in Psychology). Read this sentence:

No man is an island
No, man is an island

Just add one comma, one punctuation mark, and it changes the meaning and the philosophy of this sentence. All of us have learned and believed that man is a social animal. However, everyone needs a little "I, me, myself time." I define this as the time that you spend only with yourself—the time when you enjoy your own company, the time when you get to do your own thing.

This time, to me, is like a regular sleep schedule where the semiconscious mind combines all the data and processes it into information and logic. Similarly "I, me, myself time" helps you contemplate on yourself and Self. I have seen some people get this time in their drive to and from work. Although that is good, I do not believe it's enough.

I have a friend who is a "supermom." Professionally, she is on the rise, and personally, she has a four-year-old. She is always on the go, always slightly late for meetings, her brain working in overdrive. As I got closer to her, I asked her when was the last time she took "I, me, myself" time. With teary eyes, she replied that it's been a while.

In our world, we are always on the run, under the pressure of time, of performance, of kids, of activities. We're like ants that are always tirelessly roaming and doing something. If we take time out as an experiment, to do exactly what we wanted, I am sure we would be refreshed and recharged mentally, physically, and emotionally.

The world of meditation is one step further on this thought. We need to learn the art of being comfortable in our own skin, the art of enjoying our solitude. Have you tried to remain with yourself without watching TV or calling people and without being fearful or getting bored?

All of us need a break—need a change, need "I, me, myself" time. We should take it and give it to our near and dear ones without feeling insecure or guilty.

I enjoy "me"
Thoughts
Contemplations
Questions
Theories
Discussions

I enjoy "me"
Music
Art
Poetry
Philosophy
Nature

I enjoy "me"
And with a happy "me"
I enjoy me even more!

7. Liberty and License

A popular quote says, "Liberty is so precious that it needs to be rationed." I remember my dad and mom following this philosophy with me. During my teenage years, that felt like torture. But now, as I have seen and experienced more, I can appreciate their position.

My maternal uncle says, *"I gave you liberty but not license."* Your freedom ends where my nose begins. While my parents are the protective type, my uncle believed in letting his kids experiment—hence liberty; however, he still kept some control—hence not license.

It's funny how we, as parents, always think we can keep some control when, as each of us knows, we ourselves have broken those rules and hope we have never been caught!

Initially I think liberty is in stages: first, when one is a child, one gets a little liberty; then, during the teenage years, it's more liberty but not license; and then eventually one just takes the liberty and the license. Parents at this stage become helpless in a way, just hoping—*I hope she/he knows what she/he is doing!*

There are different parenting styles. Some parents like to protect their children and feel responsible for their behaviors forever. Others believe more in the concept of freedom, letting children fend for themselves after a certain age or taking tough action if they do not follow home rules. These parents seem to look forward to the day when their children take off for college so that they (the parents) can "get their lives back." For other parents, that is the day they feel most insecure about. Suddenly their lives are no longer centered on the children.

I do think both parents and children need to acknowledge the gifts that each one brings to the relationship. I also think the clearer the definition of "liberty" (or "license") is, the easier it is for both parties. If my parents have given me the liberty to go to a dance party, expecting me to be back by 11:00 p.m., I should not take the license to show up at 12:00 a.m. or even later!

In one of the discussions I had with a friend, Monica, she stated a great point. Most of the parents of my generation (generation X) grew up in larger families with many siblings. The attention of their parents was divided, and they weren't as involved in each child's life. In younger generations, with just one or two children, the parents have become overly attached and overly concerned and involved with their children. I sometimes sympathize with that generation of parents because they are the "sandwich" generation—relationships with their own parents were quite restrained, and they in turn are now overcompensating with their own children. Here, parents take the liberty and the license to involve themselves tremendously in their child's life.

It's all a balancing act. Both liberty and license need limits—from both parents and children!

Liberty - Or limited freedom?

License - Or control? Or discipline?
Interference - Or merely concern? Or love?

Interdependence
Codependence
And yet independent?

I strive
To keep
The balance

8. Be Sensitive, Not Touchy

To be honest, I have been given this advice many times by my well-wishers—especially my mom. Being sensitive allows one to be concerned about the person or the circumstance—one tries to understand and be compassionate to what the other person is going through. Of course, only the wearer knows where the shoe pinches; however, the least one can do is try to understand, acknowledge, and sympathize with the situation.

Being touchy, on the other hand, is going a few steps further—being overly emotional about something, taking things too personally — and usually it is over very simple things that can and should be ignored. This comes from inherent insecurity, being judgmental, or being overly attached.

I have fallen into this trap often—making a big deal of small things or being upset over minor issues! The lesson is to be conscious of what you are feeling and be sensitive. The underlying principle is simple and applies to most cases: if you think about others first, you are being sensitive; however, if you think about yourself, then you are being touchy. So, be sensitive, not touchy.

A loud word
An indifferent glance
Silence
Yes—it hurts

He
In his own world
Troubled by his past
Contemplating?
But—it still hurts!

I
The emotional self
He
The "self"-ish saint
Teaching me
To be balanced

9. Monotony

This discussion is one I have had with many people—my brother, my husband, and at times even with my own self—over a cup of coffee. Life tends to follow a routine, and routines tends to become monotonous, and monotony may lead to boredom

I live an unwanted day
I live an uninspired dream
Casually
Carelessly
Futilely

Slowly becoming a habit
Slowly ending in a state
Where it doesn't matter anymore
Emptiness grasps
My individuality
And my soul cries
"Let me free"
"Let me free"

Before I know it, I get caught in a cycle and start feeling empty and restless. Or, in some cases, I start feeling this is not enough—I need to do something more. I need to break the cycle!

With all the demands and duties of life, it is not easy to get away from a routine, but it's definitely easy to get away from monotony. As my favorite cousin Jay says, *"Bring variety to your life."* Though all days may be similar, don't let them be Xerox copies. Do something different. Let it be something even so small and mundane that it may sound humorous, but do it anyway! Take a different route to work, listen to another radio station, get out during lunchtime, and take a drive—or suddenly drop me a letter! May be, in the end these are all simple tricks to tease the mind. Believe me, it does work.

There has to be something in each day that you look forward to and are enthusiastic about. As I struggle to deal with monotony, I ask myself: what am I looking forward to today, or what fun activity am I going to do, or what is something different that I will try? As has been said, *"All you need in life is something you can be enthusiastic about."* It's easy to complain and be stagnant. It takes courage to be creative and spice up your life!

Today is anew
Like the fragrance of a rose
The rising sun smiling
Like the freshness of a daisy
The pleasant winds blowing

Today is anew
And so is this moment
And as anew is our endeavor
To Live Life
Agile and joyous
Awake and conscious
I rise to the new morning

10. Reinventing Yourself

In continuation of the last conversation, we can also break up the monotony if we keep reinventing ourselves. Reinventing implies we put ourselves in a situation where you have never been: a new place, new location, new job, and new friends—anything that is out of your comfort zone or is totally different. The best part in it is that you learn and grow.

I have done most of this. As an example of new location, I got married and came to the United States at the ripe age of twenty-nine. I love India; I had a great job, have family, friends, and relatives back there, and it is my security blanket. Following the advice from Chapter 1, The Concept of Distance, and meeting Pranav (my husband) coaxed me to take the chance and reinvent myself—go to a new country. Yes, it's worth it!

At such times you get a chance to start anew with a clean slate. And then, whenever you have a get-together and meet people from different phases of life, they will remind you how you reinvented yourself!

Reinventing yourself is an act of bravery. As my husband says, "You have to let go. Fully let go, and then enjoy the change." There are a few times in each of our lives when we are given this chance. Opportunities given need to be taken!

"LIFE: Limited In Finite Eternity" is how I define Life; hence, to make it eternal, to make life memorable and to live life, keep reinventing yourself.

A new "you"
Enhanced identity
A journey
And A Discovery

A new "you"
Today
Why wait?

A new "you"
It's for you
A gift
Of Courage

A new "you"
Still it's you
Just
Reinvented!

11. Ritual and Spiritual

Ritual and spiritual: two similar words with the same goal of being one with God and feeling His presence, and yet so different. I specifically remember a discussion with my husband, who is spiritual but does not believe in rituals. I, on the other hand, come from a ritualistic family. The concept is that all our activities should be centered on God, and so, knowingly or unknowingly, our energies—physical, mental, or spiritual—are focused on Him. However, sometimes rituals can transfer themselves into religious fanaticism. This is when, in my book, we are on dangerous ground.

Being spiritual is liberal to some extent. The argument is simple: Did God tell us to eat only these kinds of foods? Did God tell us to worship him in a certain way only? Did God tell us to go to the church or temple every Sunday? No, it wasn't God; it was a ritual invented by one of the human saints to make it simpler for us to feel God's presence. So, if you are not at that stage, you need rituals. Similarly, if you don't feel you are getting closer to God even while doing rituals, this implies that the ritual is not working for you.

The question then arises: should we take the liberty to not perform rituals? In my head, the answer is simple. Religion is a very personal feeling and should not be discussed. Religion is also very unique—to each his or her own. So both doing rituals and being spiritual can (and do) work.

A walk
To the temple
And
I am closer
To God
With each step

Discourses
Trying to define
The undefinable
Putting boundaries
On
The Ever Free

Yet
Helping me
Understand
Something
About Him

God
Enclosed in four walls?
Enclosed in an innocent smile?
Enclosed in religious texts?
Enclosed in a loving hug?

God
Within all these
And yet beyond them…

12. Compartmentalize

This is one discussion I had with my ex-boss in India. Of the many things I learned from him, this was one key lesson. I fondly used to tell him, "You taught business; I learned life." It all started when our company's contractor Patel came into the office. He had promised to complete work weeks earlier, and it still had not been completed. My boss was understandably not too happy about this. So when Patel came in, my boss gave him a piece of his mind. He has a very aggressive demeanor and is known to be ultra-disciplined. After those five minutes, there was pin-drop silence in the office. As Patel left, all of us were scared about who might be next on the "hit list."

As luck would have it, it was me! As I walked in, he was absolutely calm. We started discussing a project, and it was smooth sailing. Finally I had to ask him, "How do you do this? If I had a conversation like the one you had earlier, I would have taken everybody to task, including my husband (sorry dear!). Perhaps I would have been mad the whole day." (There is nothing a good night's sleep cannot cure!)

He said the trick is to compartmentalize your mind. You can be mad at a particular thing—an event, a thought, a particular action—but it does not mean you have to be mad at that person or at all the persons surrounding you. You are upset at one aspect of the individual but not at everything about him or her.

In reality, the compartmentalization principle applies to how we behave differently when we are with our parents, friends, peers, spouses. Each person has his or her own place—his or her own compartment. We just need to take this one step further and compartmentalize our minds for events. Once the event is over, we need to move on.

To date, I have a hard time doing this. Wisdom, however, lies in recognizing and accepting our weaknesses and working on them.

Stern face
Pulsating forehead
I only see red

All around me
Within and beyond me
I only see red

Till
I remove
These glasses

A slow smile
Enters
Encompassing
Bliss

13. Let Go and Move On

It is hard for any of us to move on. We get attached so easily—attached to a person, a thing, an idea, or even our own self. It is not necessary to always move on, provided we understand where we are and what we are compromising.

I recently had a meeting with a colleague who had a funny haircut. While talking to me, he confided that his mom had suddenly passed away. She had been staying with him for the last few months, as he had become a first-time father. On her way back to India, as she reached Hyderabad, her cab met with an accident, and she was killed on the spot. In India, it's a tradition that you shave your head when someone close, especially a family member, passes away. I had met him shortly after he returned to the United States, and hence it looked like a funny haircut.

It was shocking, and more so because I could fully relate to him. Suddenly the distance between India and the United States looked enormous! This is a hard situation, and we do not have any option but to move on.

I have caught myself multiple times getting attached to fantasies. For example, my mind wanders to what course life would have taken if I had lived in India or if I had stuck around in my first job. The trick is to identify what is fantasy versus what is real. Eventually the mind realizes the difference between fantasy and reality, and the solution is to let go and move on.

I remind myself to let go of negativities, too. Somehow, the mind always remembers a harsh word or a hostile attitude. As some saint once said, *"Nothing in this world is as bad as to abuse your mind with anger."*

I use a trick. When someone dies, in India, we have a tradition to bathe away our sorrows. I do the same in situations too I want to forget a harsh word or something negative. Sometimes one bath does not do the trick, so I take multiple baths to dissolve and bathe away the negativities, anger, and frustrations—letting go and moving on. It is not worth it to keep holding on to fantasies or hostilities.

Letting you go
My eyes shed a tear
My hopes dampen
My heart is sad

But
My dreams still exist
My faith remains
Life is not dead

You helped me move on
Learning a new life experience
Making me stronger
Pushing me
Toward a new day

14. Each Drummer Plays to His Own Beat

The inspiration for this topic came out of a discussion I had with my parents. Somehow parents, or rather we humans, have a tendency to compare ourselves to others. Rather than seeing the good, we usually end up comparing our lives to those of others see what is missing, thus creating our own misery.

However, each drummer plays to his own beat. Everyone is different, unique, and successful in his or her own area of expertise. One's sense of achievement cannot and should not be measured by whether he or she has created wealth, has social standing, is married, or is professionally successful. Certainly, if these things work out, it's a bonus. However, if one looks at the bigger picture, one's sense of achievement should be based on how one measures up to the graph of life based on one's own goals—in one's own eyes.

For example, overall in life, I want to learn how to be equanimous and to connect to the higher power. The achievements we measure people on are all temporary and can quickly change.

Hence, are our hearts and minds open to accept each drummer playing to his own beat? Or do we want to judge people on how they measure up in our book of temporary successes? Furthermore, can we encourage such drummers?

Each drummer plays to his own beat
I try to decipher
I try to comprehend
I explain
I coax
But...
Each drummer plays to his own beat

The drummer knows
His beat
I don't
I doubt his ability

He is confident of his talent
I want him to be safe
But...he wants to experiment and experience
Life

The question remains unanswered
Should I doubt my doubt?
Or should I force him to surrender?
Should I trust his judgment?
Or should I keep demanding explanations?
Should I ensure he makes no mistakes?
Or should I give him the choice to take decisions?

Black, Whites and Grays...
Each decision is circumstantial!

15. The Power Struggle: Ego Management

It is surprising how we get involved, knowingly or unknowingly, in a power struggle—especially in relationships. We want things to go our way, and we usually manipulate or convince our loved ones to succumb to our wishes. If someone opposes us, the power struggle begins! I have been on both ends—I've been the one creating the power struggle and been the one who craves power. On either end, life is not fun. It creates unnecessary pressure and often requires a moderator to settle the differences.

I usually go with one of two solutions. The first one is trying to develop a consciousness or awareness of the power struggle. At least that takes care of getting "unknowingly" caught in this. Once I am aware, all it takes is big heartedness – being generous, humor and maturity to abstain and not be affected by it. Of course, people also need to realize they are above this and power struggles are petty. The second solution is to use humor to make the other person aware of unnecessary power struggle.

I have gotten into power struggles with many people, especially within my closest circle. Perhaps if I practiced what I preach, it would help!

The other kind of power struggle is very dangerous—the one where one totally dominates the other person, not giving him or her any space to grow, wanting to dominate both thoughts and actions. Abuse is the next step here. I strongly believe that revolution or rebellion is the answer here. We give power to people to rule or dominate over us, and hence we can take the power away. We have to be mentally strong. We have to believe that life can be much more fun, instead of tolerating constant physical or mental abuse. In such cases, we will need to let the person know that we cannot and will not be dominated. Indifference works wonders, too.

I have had such a person in my life; he ran over my existence. His personality was so overpowering and charming! Furthermore, he had money. One fine day, he abused me, and I went into my "silence zone." I had seen the person talk to many others in a similar fashion. To his credit, he did realize that I was mad; and upon pestering me, he got a piece of my mind, albeit a toned-down version. It was the first time that someone made him aware; and over time, I saw a different personality emerge.

People can often tolerate your hate but not your indifference, and that's the trick.

Power struggles come down to ego management, don't they?

Ego management—managing egos
Mockery of truth?
Mockery of "the Self"?
Deep fixations?
Unexpressed emotions?
Unlived obsessions?

And I am part of the act
Of managing these mockeries
These mentalities
The power struggle

Trying to portray the truth? Really?
Playing games
Trying to become an EEM—expert in ego management

16. Get off the Roller Coaster

Recently I attended a retreat in the Ganges, MI, and the subject of discussion was "Stithpragna," which refers to a person who is stable and does not get disturbed by either the euphoria of joy or the pain of sadness. This inspired me to think, *Get off the roller coaster.*

A roller coaster signifies a lot of things, like our own fixations or emotionally draining relationships. Like a roller coaster, these swings take us up in the sky and down to the dungeons. Once you are off the roller coaster; life is on stable ground, and it helps in thinking straight.

I have seen several emotionally draining relationships where people were bound to the vague hope that things would get better. That sort of idea is good and positive; however, we still need to get off the roller coaster. We can't keep riding it and grumbling about why life or the other person is so unfair. It would help to get off and evaluate the problem practically with the head, not the heart.

The point is that when we are fixated on an idea, we put ourselves on a roller coaster and experience wild mood swings. The trick is to be determined, but to act as an observer. Watch the roller coaster. Be aware of it. If possible, enjoy it, but don't get carried away to the highs or the lows by it—and if you are not confident, simply get off the roller coaster.

So, stop being a victim. Take charge of your emotions—your attitude and your life. Be an observer and enjoy!

I want to be married at twenty-five
And I want to have children before thirty
And I want to be in love soon...
There...I am on the roller coaster now

I want to leave him
But I don't want to hurt him
And I know I should leave him
There....I am on the roller coaster now

It's been a crazy ride
I am scared, shaken, and unstable
I wonder at and admire people who enjoy roller coasters
I am not one who enjoys them
I am getting off...
I will remain on the ground...
I will Take Charge!

17. Nonviolence

My brother and I were having a discussion about the Indian independence struggle. There were various strategies used. One was using violence to get attention, fight authority, and prove a point. Another approach was the nonviolence preached by Mahatma Gandhi, where the basic principle was strong will and a stubborn belief in being truthful and tolerant—being nonviolent. It's a simple term, but it's so hard to practice.

Imagine you are on the freeway, and the driver ahead of you is driving slowly in the fast lane. Your first urge is to honk at him. Nonviolence does not just mean nonviolent actions; it also means nonviolent thoughts—nonviolence of the mind. It means having a forgiving, tolerant attitude. Imagine that instead of us, it was Lord Buddha driving. Would he have honked, or would he have just been patient and given a mind-capturing smile?

We all have irritants in life, both minor and major. We may be irritated by our relatives, acquaintances, neighbors, strangers, health issues, and even ourselves! The idea is "Titiksha"—being tolerant and enduring of whatever comes our way, without being affected by it. If we believe in nonviolence, we need to try to start thinking nonviolence from our minds, too. Just because we are not going out of our way to harm somebody does not mean we are practicing nonviolence.

There will come a stage when we are at peace with ourselves and the world around us. Then there will be nothing that can disturb that peace; it will pain us if we even unknowingly hurt any living thing, and the core principles of being truthful and strong-willed will lead the way toward becoming truly nonviolent.

Bombed buildings
Eerie streets
Bloodshed and death
Why?

In the era of short memories
Is this really worth it?

Overcrowded trains
Running late
A push from a stranger
The "f***" word
Why?
What did it prove?

A nagging pain
Limiting
Anger
And helplessness
Did this help?
Why?

Buddha
Enjoying the irritants
Living nonviolence
Peaceful
And
Complete

18. The Old Man's Syndrome

Here is a thought-provoking statement: "If you are still talking about what you did yesterday, you haven't done anything much today." We all have a habit of reminiscing about the past. However, if that is all we do, we have what I call the "old man's syndrome," implying that these memories are all merely stories of the past.

While thinking about this one day, I came across Paolo Coelho's book *The Valkyries*. Books can sometimes be better intellectual friends. In it, he says that when we really reach that age, the past is more secure than the future. Hence, we live in the past through "old man's syndrome."

However, although the past may be more secure, we do have the present and at least some part of the future. It would be more fun if we could keep living in the present. As my husband mentioned the other day, it's all about a struggle to be relevant.

I dislike how it makes me feel when people give up on life and what it can offer, succumbing to the old man's syndrome. The game is not over till it's really over. Each second is a gift that needs to be enjoyed.

The worst part about the old man's syndrome is that you keep telling the same stories over and over again. Well, that is what happens when you only have the past to talk about. There may be a lot of wisdom hidden in it, but after a point, it just gets monotonous.

A funny thing about the old man's syndrome is that it strikes over and over; you just delve deeper and deeper into the past. I remember my grandma talking about events that had happened fifty years ago—all about family feuds. None of those people were present—or, sadly, even alive—when all this was being narrated, yet her bad memories were.

The lesson is that although advancing in years is a fact of life, something that is going to happen (and something that we pray should happen, unless we are to meet God much sooner than expected!), we should be conscious and cautious not to be caught up in the old man's syndrome. We should continue to live life with zest, creating new stories and turning the present into unforgettable memories.

As time knocks on my door
I want to be remembered
As a wise old person
With stories old and new
With life's lessons

Some with adventures
Some fun—some funny
Some that have happened
Some that still remain to be created
Some sad
But no stories with grudges
Even though I lived it, I don't need to remember it

Stories of the past
And of the present
And dreams of the future

The old man's syndrome
For the old man
Is fun (hopefully)

But I promise
To live in the present

19. "You" Attitude

Having a "you" attitude means that instead of centering the world on "I" and "me," we center it around "you." It implies that I think of you first, before I think of myself. It implies that I am considerate and focused on what's happening in your life and with your mind instead of being focused on myself. I have always strongly believed in having a "you" attitude. It is a great foundation to build relationships on.

Face it—everyone loves his or her own self. With a "you" attitude, we can also become a part of another person—an extension of the person. I tend to refer to my husband as an extension of myself. It's his "you" attitude towards me that he goes above and beyond by specially taking care of the little things. How I appreciate it!

It is hard to maintain "you" attitude. We have to think of the other person first, understand his or her likes and dislikes—and especially what he or she expects from us. We have to train and channel our minds for this.

What always surprises and saddens me is when I don't see people reflecting or reciprocating the "you" attitude. Once one achieves a certain height in spiritualism, this doesn't matter, but for me it still does. I have a few friends who, whenever we meet, only talk about their own lives, families, careers, and time management. In an hour of conversation, there are just five minutes devoted to talking about my life. With such friends, one starts becoming the "Agony Aunt." Eventually, unless one reaches a higher spiritual stage, the relationship suffers or becomes convoluted and single-sided.

I always laugh when I think of "you" attitude and parents. In the beginning, when a child is young, all the parents have is "you" attitude—sometimes over-the-top "you" attitude. Did my baby eat? Did my baby sleep? Did my baby poop? Is my baby sleeping ok?

As the child grows into an adult, this attitude gets converted many times into management by guilt. "I did so much for you, how can you not do this for me?" While it's a fact that we can never repay our parents for the love and care they gave us, it is also humorous to see "you" attitude turn into "I/me" attitude. I wonder why we as humans and specially as parents always need to be reassured that we are loved.

"You" attitude is an art; it's an attitude we all should learn and develop. It develops our emotional quotient and teaches us to be empathetic—and yet, is it right to maintain a "you" attitude twenty-four-seven? Do all people deserve to be given a "you" attitude?

I think "you"
Your day
Your struggles
Your joys
Your life

I try
To make you smile
To hold your hand
To be with you
For you

I think "you"
Can you
At least for a little while
Try to think "me"?

20. Contentment and Complacency

I came across an article on greed and avarice in a book, *Saadhak Sanjivani*, by Swami Ramsukhdasji. While he was discussing how to be content with what we have without succumbing to greed, I started wondering how we might differentiate between contentment and complacency.

"Each man reaches his highest level of incompetence." Does that mean that when we reach that stage, we are both content and complacent?

Whether it is contentment or complacency is a question each person has to answer for themselves. There are many times when people may think you are complacent or lazy, but do you also think the same? Or are you a part of the divine experience—experiencing him at each moment? It's all about self-reflection.

Many times, with the outlook of contentment, we stop trying to improve. In the end, we are fooling no one else but ourselves. If it is indeed a veil, then we need to know and acknowledge the same. But the humorous part is that the state of mind may also change—today you may sincerely be content, but after a few days you may feel complacent. After all, we are all blessed (or cursed) with restless souls. As said by Fernando Pessoa in *The Book of Disquiet*:

> My soul is impatient with itself, as with a bothersome child; its restlessness keeps growing and is forever the same. Everything interests me, but nothing holds me. I attend to everything, dreaming all the while....I'm two, and both keep their distance— Siamese twins that aren't attached.

Hence this restlessness feeds both contentment and complacency.

My answer to this question—contentment or complacency—came to me when I was sharing a cup of coffee with Pranav, my husband. The coffee was good, but it could have been better. Hence, I was content at that point in time, but not complacent. The next time, I would be working harder to get it right.

There are three basic paths of spiritualism according to Hinduism: knowledge, action, and devotion. The highest achievement in the path of knowledge is omniscience and omnipresence—visualization of the divine resplendence. In the path of action, it is achievement of constant happiness; and in the path of devotion, it is God experience. If that's the goal, we can be content with baby steps, but we cannot afford to be complacent.

I am content
I have earned some fame
A name
Some money
A lovable honey
Traveled to places
Enjoyed the faces
Smiled a lot
Relished the gifts life brought

I guess
I should be content
Should I?

21. Don't Give up Just Because You Think It's Tough

This was advice given by a close friend. I was trying to make a crucial decision about whether to leave something, and he said, "Don't give up just because you think it is tough." If you give up, there is the possibility that you will regret it later; you may think that if you had tried a little harder, done a little more, life would have been better. Of course, the corollary to this is, "If you don't succeed at first, try again and again and again and then give up—there is no use being a damn fool about it!"

Yet, "Success is the best revenge." What this says to me is that everything is situation based. Let's not give up on things that have a longer impact on your life—pursuing an education, looking for a spouse, making an effort to get pregnant. In cases like these, we may someday be filled with regrets, a feeling of weakness for our own self, our mind, and our will. The reason for not giving up on long-term impacts is that if we make choices, we have to accept the consequences, and these consequences are long term.

For short-term things, I have personally given up on things—or rather, I haven't ventured into trying many of them—like playing sports and scuba diving. For example when we went to Hawaii, my husband tried to teach me to swim with the waves. I tried a few times and then gave up. It would have been better if I hadn't given up; I would have had a better story to tell. Oh well!

So, let's not give up on long-term impact issues just because we think it's tough!

It's tough
But I am tougher

It's painful
But I am stronger

It's persistent
But I am patient

It wants to make me lose
But I am a winner

It's impossible
But I excel at possibilities

It can kill
But not my will

It wants me to succumb
But it doesn't know
"I don't give up"

22. The Voices of Silence

The inspiration of this topic came from a short story, "Year of Silence," by Kevin Bruckheimer. The author writes about how gripping and involving both silence and voices can be.

Silence is very meditative. It forces one to self-reflect. In the moment of silence, it seems like the whole world is comprised of you and Him. However, silence can also be shallow. It can be easily disturbed by a little sound—a little voice—and you are then pulled away into that thought trail of why the voice, and where's the voice coming from. Silence can also be eerie, and voices can be unpleasant, too.

I like silence—the quiet—especially early in the morning. It gives me a sense of peace and of connecting with myself. A further challenge is to silence the mind even if things are externally loud. That is a battle worth winning.

When I came to the United States from India, the biggest difference I observed was the silence. India is always bursting with energy, people, and lots and lots of sounds, such as the sounds of traffic, cyclists, barking dogs, honking, your doorbell, your cell phone, people selling vegetables and fruits, or the cow mooing. Here in the United States, you hardly hear any sounds, although you may hear the background noise of the freeway or the voices on TV.

I guess it's all about balancing silence with voices. In silence, you want to hear your soul, so you still want the voice of your soul. In sound, you want to experience life and its nuances; and yet what you want is to self-reflect on the voices. In both cases, though, you are just trying to connect with yourself...silencing the mind and listening to the voice of the soul.

The voices of silence
The silent voices

Sounds....Melody
Noises ....Activity
Shouts....Chaos

Silence ....Peace
Quiet......Calm
Hushed....Eerie....death

Voices
Unwanted disturbance

Silence
Welcome restlessness

A longing
To hear the voices
Of silence

23. The Truth of Lies

This conversation was inspired by a book about a guy who constantly makes up stories—lies, rather—about his life. He does it so naturally that sometimes it scares even him.

It's not that I have never lied at all or exaggerated some situations, but the sort of lying the book discusses is at a whole different level. It's like lying at every point or every hour of the day.

I wonder how people do it—and I wonder more *why* we lie. Is it insecurity? Is it fear? Is it guilt? Is it that we are trying to protect someone? Is it a lack of courage? Is it just that we have built up an image of ourselves and so we use lies to prove it—adding one more hypocrisy to this hypocritical world?

I feel that if we get to the bottom of the lie, we will realize its futility. Lies can be simple or complex. Simple lies are the excuses we make, knowing fully well in our heads that they are excuses. Complex lies are the ones where we deceive ourselves depicting hypocrisy. I am always afraid of these, for "if you wear a mask too long, it becomes your face."

I am a big proponent of speaking the truth. I have found that truth gives me a lot of power and courage. It forces me to check my assumptions and to introspect. It also forces me to develop respect for others, to trust them, to understand them, and to accept them. I would rather know the harsh truth than nice-sounding lies. At least with the truth, I can estimate the consequences. With lies, it will be a bigger shock.

So, the next time you think about lying, think about why you are doing it. Is it really worth it? If possible, choose to be silent rather than lie, or choose not to give explanations. Truth has a lot of power, and we should develop the courage to live with the truth.

The truth
Of lies
Hides
In them

As
I become
Aware
I realize
Peace is
Where truth lies!

24: Nothing Changes Life Like Death

The title itself, stated by my husband, is so paradoxical! The thought was inspired when our close family friend, a seventy-four-year-old, lost his forty-two-year-old son to a heart attack. For the last decade, the father had devoted his life to the pursuit of spiritualism and service of humanity. He had spent hours preaching, and now suddenly, all had changed. Yes, nothing changes life more than death. The son was a businessperson, and now the father, the preacher, manages this business for twelve hours a day! All his dreams of retirement, of travels, of seeing his son grow old and take care of him, are now shattered. The life he had lived was totally different from the life he is living now.

This just shows us how volatile life can be, how destiny can take a turn and take you for a ride. In Indian scriptures, there are various kinds of detachments. One is when you are truly detached from earthly concerns, or rather attached to the Supreme Being. In this kind of detachment, your world is centered on Him; and you are not affected by joy or sorrow, life or death, as it is all temporary.

The other detachment is what we feel right now—after reading this, after attending someone's memorial service, where we feel the fragility of life, where we question the purpose of life, where we crave for something eternal. However, this is short-lived. As soon as some days pass, and we get back to our routine, we forget all about this detachment.

I must say that the seventy-four-year-old family friend has practiced what he preached. He is stable. He accepts his son's death as a decision God made for his own well-being and is confident his son is in a better place. His life has sure changed, but this too is God's will.

Yes, nothing changes life more than death.

Death has promised to come
To elevate us from everything
Memories – Ailments – Relationships and Life

Life has promised to stay
To make us learn and make
Memories – Journeys – Relationships and Progeny

In this constant cycle
Of uncertain life and certain death
We hope to find
The purpose and
Enjoy
The journey

25. What Are You Scared Of?

This topic came from a conversation with my mentor, Carolyn. The conversation began when I told my mentor that I intend to eventually be self-employed. She coaxed me to think and asked a great question: "If you had a guarantee that you would not fail what would you do?" This is a profound question. The corollary is this: What are you scared of?

We all have various fears and insecurities; some are logical, and others are merely in the psyche. We all have experienced the irrational fears— for example, for no good reason, we are afraid of the dark or of shadows. There are logical fears, too, of choices we make and consequences. Is this the right relationship? Is this the right career move? Is this the right investment?

So, the first step is knowing *what* you are scared of, but the next—and bigger—step is figuring out *how* you are going to address it and being aware of the behavior that fear is driving. Are you going to live in fear and just accept the consequences? Accept the status quo? Are you going to build some sort of safety net? Are you going to move forward and live courageously on the edge and take the risk of failing?

These choices exist, and all choices are ours. Whatever decision we make, we need to ensure that regret does not take the place of dreams. Being scared is OK, but letting fear overrule you is sad.

The risk and reward theory does seem to be applicable at all places. All successful people have failed. I remember I once asked my ex-boss in India when he earned his first million dollars, and he replied, "I lost a million dollars before I earned them." He used to manage a company that went bankrupt. He then started a new business manufacturing toothbrushes and made his millions.

It's very easy to be fearful and to stay in our comfort zone. The adventure begins when you face your fears.

I am captured by my
Fears
Uncertainty
Insecurity

I am captured
By my present

I am captured
By known days

I am captured
By predictability

I do enjoy it
The comfort zone
The known faces
The prison

I am scared of
The free world
As I have only seen
The prison

26: Nothing Is Better Than Nonsense

These words of wisdom are from J. Krishnamurthy: "Something is better than nothing, but nothing is better than nonsense." I heard this from one of our family friends. I have loved this line, and musing over this book took me back down memory lane to this discussion over a cup of coffee.

Indeed, nothing is better than nonsense. We all have had days or hours within the day when we have killed time. Watching a useless movie or a show, participating in an unproductive and unnecessary conversation, or reading a thoughtless book, entertaining the idea that we are at least doing *something*...but nothing is better than nonsense!

It would have been better if we had just sat in silence for a little bit, quieting our minds. I am sure we would have come up with more interesting and energetic things to do. Doing wasteful things not only wastes time in the first place, it also has a lingering effect—"energy drains," as some people call it. The measure of whether you enjoy an activity is how you feel after doing it. Do you feel drained, or do you feel charged? If you feel charged, even though the activity may be tedious, that's the way to go. If you feel drained, and you keep on doing it, it will just take you down into more negativity like feeling tired, being grumpy, feeling guilty, and even feeling mentally and physically sick! Hence, nothing is better than nonsense.

One trick that I have found useful when I am in a really productive, creative mind-set is to make a list of things I would do if I had time on my hands—very specific things. For example, I want to read *Jonathan Livingston Seagull* by Richard Bach, or I want to watch a particular movie, or I would like to paint a picture of the sunset. Then, when I am searching for activities, getting restless, or getting bored, I look at that list and see what I feel like doing.

I know we all go through phases of life, and I know that we all are unstill souls, always craving something more; yet nothing is better than nonsense.

Let's do something
Anything
At least one thing
Nothing?

I am bored
And tired
I want to talk
And be quiet

My mind roams
Finding faults
A constant chatter
Of something
Of anything
Of everything

I crave for
Nothing
Away from the chatter
Away from the nonsense
Away from everything
Into
Nothing
For
Nothing
Enjoying nothing?

27: Loneliness and Solitude

My brother once said, "Convert the agony of loneliness into the bliss of solitude." Both loneliness and solitude are effectively the same state, and yet the attitude and emotion attached with these are vastly different. One is agony, and one is bliss! What a paradox!

I do believe that one should be comfortable with oneself is one's own skin, enjoying their own company and solitude. I am always amazed by people who can talk endlessly and by people who constantly need to be on the run, constantly inventing unnecessary activity as a farce of "being busy" to be away from oneself, away from being lonely.

Well, I do agree that these tricks work. However, I always ask the question: Why are you feeling lonely? Why are you feeling "less blessed"? Why are you afraid of doing nothing, being idle, and enjoying the solitude?

On the other hand, we have heard of saints who have spent their entire lives alone in pious places, chanting the name of the Lord. They are engrossed and at one with the Self. They truly experience the bliss of solitude.

I do enjoy my own company. In solitude, I like to challenge my mind toward creativity; I like to enjoy the quiet, hearing little sounds; watching the sky, the snow-clad trees, watching the stillness, hearing my own breathing, and feeling blessed, feeling thankful to be living.

I strongly feel that each one of us should have a hobby, a passion—or multiple hobbies and passions—to keep us going. Outside of work, we need to have some other identity, too—something else that drives us, something else that keeps us comfortable in our own skin, worthy enough to experience the bliss of solitude.

Solitude
Peace
Undisturbed
Profound
Contemplating
Silent
Loving
Natural
Serene
Somber
An experience of bliss

28. The Buck Stops Here

It is so easy for us to blame events, circumstances, persons, politicians, nature—you name it—for whatever situation we are in. However, I have always believed and tried to live by the belief that the buck stops here.

I am responsible for my own happiness, for my own bliss, and for what I choose to do with the situation I am in. I can either choose to play the "blame game" or to do something about it.

It's funny how in the corporate world, you wait for your boss (or boss's boss) to give you answers or tell you to do something. However, if we all believe the buck stops with us, we will work and find solutions instead of waiting on someone else to do it. As Sri Sri Ravi Shankar says, *"Responsibility is owning what is missing, what is there, and even what is possible."*

I think it's better to believe that the buck does stop here. What would I do if I were the boss? How would I change the situation? What is my internal coach telling me? What is within my control?

The concept comes down to "owning". If we think we own it, we will take responsibility for it.

The question is what's stopping us?   Let the buck stop here! Make the buck stop here!

I can find a hundred excuses
I can find someone to blame
I can simply shrug my shoulders
Wouldn't it be a shame?

I can get some direction
Or I can choose a path
The buck stops here
Surely is the path

Own the situation
And own up
You are in it for a reason
So chin up

Show up and
Drive the change
Let the buck stop here
Don't let things remain the same

29. The Bumblebee Flies Anyway

The topic is a title of a movie I watched. The concept was of mind over matter. The story revolved around a group of kids who were terminally ill. The idea was to erase the memory of their minds, so they would think everything was normal. Lo and behold, their bodies started behaving normally! The movie director linked it back to the bumblebee. Due to its weight and aerodynamics, the bumblebee should not be able to fly. However, the bumblebee does not know that, so it flies anyway!

Too many times, I have limited myself. The reminder for me is, "Argue for your limitations and sure enough they are yours," a statement by Richard Bach. We think we can only reach a certain point. We come up against artificial barriers or are bound by the "rules" we have been told.

However, time and again it has been proven that the mind is above matter, and the mind can even modify matter. It does require a forceful will, focused attention, and a strong belief. For the yogis or people who have survived the odds, I am convinced, it's mind over matter.

Although a bumblebee is not how I picture myself, I think the lesson it teaches is incredible. Even the bumblebee flies! It cannot fly like an eagle, but it flies.

So next time I start to say, "I can't do it," I am going to stop and think. Am I limiting myself? Am I saying "no" just for convenience?

I didn't know
I couldn't fly
I saw wings
I saw birds and
I flew

Maybe not as high
Maybe not as far
But I flew
Effortlessly

Now, I know
I cannot fly
The knowledge is no good
I still fly
But
It takes a lot of effort

30. What Would You Put in Your "Memory Palace"?

This topic arose from a book I was reading, *The Memory Palace*, by Mira Bartok. The book is about a child growing up with a schizophrenic mother. The child is always torn between the love she feels versus the practicality of living with someone who doesn't make sense 90 percent of the time. Hard decisions! In any case, she uses a technique called "Memory Palace" to organize her memories, building each room of the palace with memories of events, nature, paintings, music, and so on so she can always remember them.

I thought about this topic more one day while I was talking with my brother about learning how to decide what to remember and what to forget. We all have been haunted by bad memories—harsh words, inappropriate behaviors, grudges. Typically these are things that have happened in the past. I ask myself, is it worth remembering, or is it worth forgetting?

The story of, Socrates, is apt when he asks his student to only tell him things that are (a) true, (b) useful, and (c) beneficial

So the question here is this: What would be worth remembering? And what would you and I put in our memory palaces? What would each room look like, smell like, sound like, and feel like? The author of *The Memory Palace* uses the memory palace to escape into the world of happy moments. I really like the idea. When I have a hard day or am haunted by unpleasant memories, all I need to do is take a stroll in my memory palace, and it will make me smile.

A walk down memory lane
In my memory palace
School friends
Silly jokes
Jest and fun

A second room
Another era
Lovers
And the ocean
Sunsets and shells
The smell of the sea...ahhh

Another room
Little feet
Running about
Naughty eyes
And tight hugs

I walk by the rooms
Peeping in them
Smiling
Reliving the moment
In my memory palace

31. You Are...Am I (URMI)? I Am...Are You?

The most fun in my name is that it can be deciphered in different ways!

Yesterday I was watching a documentary on the life of Buddha. Before becoming enlightened, or "Buddha," he too, like us, was confused as to why there is so much suffering in the world. In his quest, he first devoted time to yogic practices under guidance from a teacher. However, he realized this was not giving him any answers. Then he chose to try asceticism, where one tries to get above and beyond the body and its needs. So for a while, he was eating just a grain of rice and drinking his own urine—to the extent that he was on the verge of death due to starvation. By God's grace a lady came by and offered him food, and during the process he realized asceticism was not the answer for him. He spent six years following those two paths.

Meanwhile, he had a vision where he realized he was happiest at a time when he felt connected with all living beings—like "Sarvatma bhava." So he sat under a Bodhi tree and didn't leave it till he found his answer. He decided to "look within" and become enlightened—and he became the Buddha.

As I think about this, I think about enlightenment and humbly my name - You are...am I? It reminds me of the concept of oneness with God and the soul being eternal. The question addresses whether I have that consciousness all the time. You—You the Self—the Supreme—You "are"; and I, I am a part of you—but do I remember that all the time? Hence the question: am I?

Ideally it would be, "You are, and I am too." That's the desired state. And if that's the case, why am I so bothered with petty events, things, or people? Why is it so hard to find my true nature?

For those who have successfully done this—the saints, Buddha, the karma yogis—the question they have is, "I am, are you?"

I
That's me
Me - the body
Me - the soul
Me - The Self

And
I am
Need I say more?

Are you?
Do I really care?
Can I help change it?
To
You are
You are too

Now, you are
But am I?
*When did **I am** become am I?*

The consciousness struggle
Continues
Someday
Yes, someday
It will be
I am

32. "No" Is Just Another Answer

I have a problem. I dislike debates, conflicts, and negotiations. Somehow it always feels like a power struggle, where you are directly or indirectly working on or coaxing someone to give in and live by your idea. However, I know not everything is like that. Not everything is a power struggle; sometimes a debate can just be a different point of view. Also, all answers cannot and should not be a "yes"; hence, "no" is just another answer.

The issue for people like me is that we invest our egos, our passion, our total in it; and when the answer "yes" does not happen, we feel dejected. I tell myself to remember the Gita. "Do your duty, and let Him decide what's best for you." The answer "no" is His decision and if I trust Him I should lovingly accept it. Lord, help me to accept that no is just another answer!

In the ancient times, people held a lot of spiritual debates. If all of the participants considered this a yes/no approach, so many theories and principles wouldn't have materialized. We need "no" to be an answer to find a better solution or substantiate the argument. Let "no" be an answer too.

Also, not every argument means it's a life-or-death situation. It may simply be a different point of view at that moment in time. Why do I take it more seriously than necessary? Why am I getting stuck on it? It's OK for "no" to be an answer.

The last tip I use for myself is to continue to think of the bigger picture. Maybe I am upset with the answer "no" right now—today—but as I think about it, will I be upset tomorrow? After a month? After a year? After ten years? Will I even remember this event? Let me free myself! "No" is just another answer, and so is "yes"!

Yes and no
Yay and nay
Just a set
Of answers

Nothing so absolute
Nothing so material
Just a set
Of answers

Accept both answers
Enjoy both answers
No is just another answer
and so is Yes

33: The Clock Bias

The basis of this discussion arose from Pranav, my husband, as he celebrated his fortieth birthday. The clock bias! It's funny when you suddenly realize that you <u>are</u> forty (or two years away from forty), and that feeling is what I call the Clock Bias.

Age is surely in the mind. Although the body may do its thing eventually, age is more in the mind, especially when you are healthy. On my recent trip to India, I noticed that age catches up to people faster than here in United States. I wonder if this clock bias comes from India's overpopulation, traffic, stress, need to get ahead and stay ahead, or from the innate attitude of retirement at sixty and spending time depicting rituals.

The clock bias is funny, too. For those of us who married late, we feel younger in a way, as our children are younger. For my friends who married young and have kids in high school, it seems like they feel older (to me at least!). It is a bias, though—just a bias.

As I think of clock bias, I think of what my seventy-year-old self would tell me now? What advice would age and wisdom pass on? Would my seventy-year-old self be happy with me, or would she tell me to do something different? Take more risks? Spend more time doing spiritual practices? Live more, laugh more, enjoy the togetherness, and not think of clock bias?

Captured in the clock
My days
My years

Each passing year
A new number
A bigger number

Countdown begins
To the end
Or to the beginning?

There is no fun
Being captured
By this clock

Each moment
Is new
Is a blessing

Each moment
Holds a secret
Of eternality

34: The Elusive Six Hundred

This thought came from my boss, Becky, after she attended a presentation and was explaining the crux of it to us. The average person speaks about 150 words per minute. Research shows that humans can hear approximately 750 words per minute. So what happens to the other six hundred words each minute when somebody is speaking to us or when we are speaking? That's what some experts have dubbed the "elusive six hundred."

I have experienced this umpteen times, and I am sure you have too—right from our tender age in classrooms up till the present.

The important question, though, is where we are spending our elusive six hundred. Am I spending it on conspiracy theories? Reading into a person's life? Reading into why someone is saying something? Or am I spending the elusive six hundred thinking about positive things or doing mantra recitation?

As I think about it more, it seems God gave us the elusive six hundred so we can feel connected to him all the time. And I know the elusive six hundred in this case are pretty elusive!

It also reminds me of the art of listening as well as the art of engaging somebody to ensure that the elusive six hundred does not cause unnecessary distractions.

I said
He heard
Did he?
Did he listen?

Same complaints
"You are not listening"
But I am!

It's this elusive six hundred
That gets in my way
And in yours too
But
I don't complain

Made in the USA
Monee, IL
29 November 2022

18999476R00049